ISBN NO. 978-1-7361397-1-4

This book is dedicated to my father, Marlon Brando Nash Sr., who passed away 2/2/19. He always believed me & my talent. He was my biggest fan. He was an entrepreneur for many years, & was my biggest inspiration in chasing my dream to do what I love. I learned so many things about food through his raw, untapped kitchen savvy, that was nourished from his interest in the culinary world. These recipes are some of favorite things that I would make in his small kitchen, that made him feel like he was in a five star restaurant. These recipes are a piece of me, my passion for cooking, & cooking for people. Cook like it's your last meal!

CHEF MARLO

# YOU SEE *the* FLAVOR

COOKBOOK VOL.I

# Menu of Contents

CHEF

MARLO

Coffee Rubbed Lamb

# Coffee Rubbed Lamb

Ingredients
- 1 New Zealand Frenched Lamb Rack
- 1 tbsp of Dijon mustard
- 2 tbsp of olive oil

For Coffee Rub
- 2 tablespoons finely grinded coffee beans
- 1 teaspoon chipotle powder
- 1 teaspoon onion powder
- 1 teaspoon garlic powder
- 1 teaspoon smoked paprika
- 1 teaspoon of cocoa powder
- 1 ½ teaspoon of kosher salt
- ½ teaspoon of pepper
- 1 teaspoon of cumin

Directions
- Preheat oven to 400 degrees
- Trim excess fat and silver skin from lamb rack
- Rub lamb rack with Dijon mustard & 1 tablespoon of coffee rub
- Preheat olive oil in Sautee pan on medium to high heat, until pan begins slightly smoking.
- Sear lamb rack in sauté pan for 2 min per side and move directly into oven.
- Total cook time for lamb: 8 min for rare. 10 min medium rare. 12 min for medium. 14 min for medium well. 16 min for well. 18 min for well done.
- Allow lamb to rest for 10 min before cutting.

# Garlic Sautéed Green Beans

### Ingredients

- 1 pound of fresh Haricot Vert or French green beans
- 3 cloves of fresh garlic, thinly sliced
- 2 tbsp olive oil
- ¼ tsp red pepper flakes
- salt & pepper to taste

## CHEF'S SUGGESTIONS:

*Blanching water should be about 1 cup of salt per gallon of water. You can also add ingredients such as sliced almonds or roasted/sliced red bell peppers to enhance flavors & textures.*

### Preparation

• Blanch green beans in generously salted water for 6 to 7 minutes or until tender

• Drain water from green beans and immediately transfer into ice water bath until completely cool.

• Heat olive oil in sauté pan over medium high heat, add garlic and allow garlic to cook until edges start to turn golden brown. Add green beans and pepper flakes and sauté for 2-3 minutes. Season to taste with salt & pepper.

# Oven Roasted Potatoes

## Ingredients

- ½ of pound of red potato quartered
- ½ of pound of golden potato quartered
- 4 tablespoons of olive oil
- 1 tablespoon of chopped parsley
- Salt and pepper to taste

### Preparation

- Preheat oven to 350 degrees

- Toss cut potatoes w/ olive oil salt and pepper.

- Spread evenly onto a baking sheet

- Roast for 15 minutes

- Rotate potatoes and roast for another 15 minutes, ensuring the edges are golden brown.

- Tossed cooked potatoes with parsley & serve.

 CHEF'S SUGGESTIONS:

*Make sure potatoes are dry before roasting. You can add an extra zing to these potatoes when pairing them with other dishes by, adding an herb blend(thyme, rosemary, and/or sage), adding a heavy sprinkling of parmesan cheese, or a pesto once potatoes are cooked.*

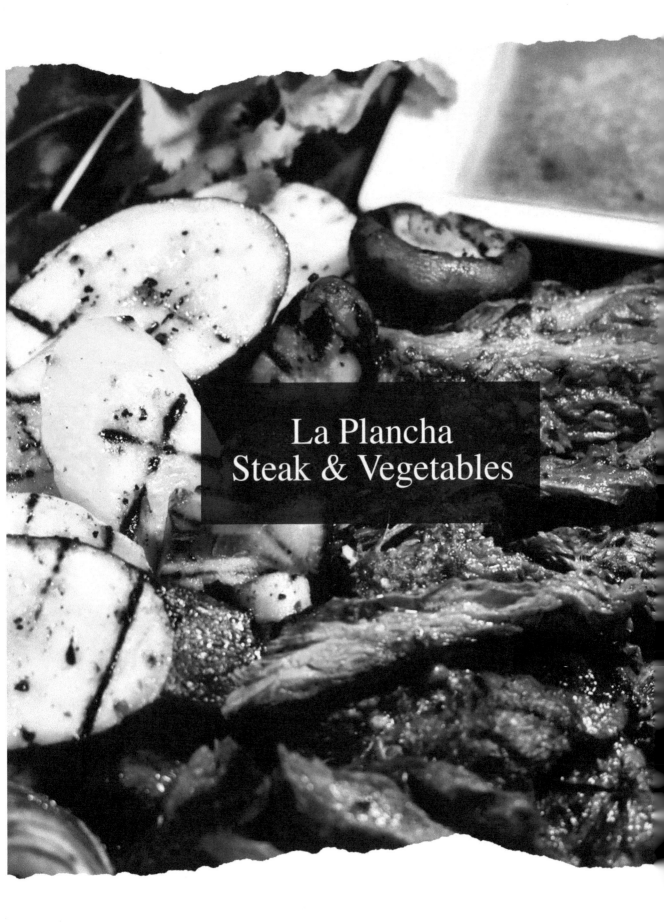

# La Plancha
# Steak & Vegetables

# La Plancha Steak & Vegetables

## Ingredients

- 1 pound of skirt steak
- 4 tbsp Salsa Verde (see page)
- 1 large zucchini, 1inch bias cut
- 1 large yellow squash, 1 inch bias cut
- 8oz mushrooms, cleaned
- 1 red onion, cut into ½ in rings
- 4 tbsp olive oil
- salt & pepper to taste

## CHEF'S SUGGESTIONS:

*Garnish steak with more salsa verde. Salsa verde is also a nice accompaniment for the grilled veggies. This dish is also delicious with grilled tortillas, or Spanish style rice.*

## Directions

• Remove any excess membrane or silver skin from skirt steak. Marinate steak with 4 tbsp of salsa verde, for minimum of 30 minutes up to overnight.

• Preheat grill top pan on high heat, until it is smoking.

• Season veggies with 3 tbsp of olive oil and salt & pepper to taste.

• Grill zucchini, onions, and squash for 2-3min per side. Start in a 10:00 position then move to a 2:00 position after 1 minute before flipping to the other side. Grill 2 minutes more & remove from grill.

• Grill Mushrooms until tender, moving around the grill every 45 seconds to cook all sides.

• Place steak on hot grill and cook for 2-3 min per side, ensuring a good amount char on both sides. Total cook time 4-5 min: rare;  5-6min medium rare;  6-7min medium; 7-8min medium well, 9-10 min well done. Allow steak to rest for 10 minutes before slicing and serving.

Pan Roasted Salmon
w/ caramelized fennel &
marinated tomato salad

# Pan Roasted Salmon w/ caramelized fennel & marinated tomato salad

### Ingredients

*for salad*
- 1 pound of cherry tomatoes, cut in half length-wise
- ¼ cup sherry wine vinegar
- 2tbs parsley, rough chopped
- ½ cup of olive oil, & 2 tbsp
- 2 cloves of garlic, chopped
- 1 medium shallot, small dice
- 1tsp red pepper flake
- 1tsp Italian blend seasoning
- 2 cups of arugula
- 1 bulb of fennel, core removed, sliced quarter inch thick. Reserve fennel fronds.

*for salmon*
- 1 pound of Salmon; 2-8oz cuts
- 1 tbsp of Dijon mustard
- Salt & pepper to taste

Directions *for salad*

• In bowl combine sherry wine vinegar and a ½ cup of olive oil, whisk vigorously about 30 seconds to combine. Add tomatoes, shallots, garlic, parsley, pepper flake, italian seasoning, and salt & pepper to taste. Allow to marinate for 30 minutes, up to overnight.

• Pre heat oven to 400 degrees

• Toss sliced fennel slices, 2 tbsp of olive oil

# Pan Roasted Salmon w/ caramelized fennel & marinated tomato salad

Directions continued:

• Spread evenly on a baking sheet, and roasting for 30-40 minutes, or until fennel is caramelized, tender, & sweet. Allow to cool.

• In a bowl mix 2 cups of arugula, ¼ cup of marinated tomatoes with dressing, & ¼ cup of fennel. Mix gently & serve.

Directions *for salmon*

• Rub salmon filets with Dijon mustard and season with salt & pepper to taste.

• Heat sauté pan with 2 tbsp of olive oil, until gently smoking.

• Place salmon in pan, flesh side down & cook 3-4 minutes per side.

• Remove from pan and serve with fennel salad. Garnish salmon with tomato marinade andt reserved fennel fronds.

## CHEF'S SUGGESTIONS:

*This dish can also be made with shrimp or chicken, cook times will vary.*

# Potato Salad Trifecta

Ingredients (Yields 4 Servings)
- ½ pound sweet potatoes, peeled & ½ inch dice
- ½ pound red skin potatoes, ½ inch dice
- ½ pound gold potatoes, ½ inch dice
- 1 cup roma tomatoes, seeded & ¼ inch dice
- 1 cup red onions, ¼ inch dice
- 1 cup of roasted red pepper sauce (see page)
- 3 tbsp parsley, rough chopped

Directions
• Blanch potatoes in a pot of salted, gently boiling water, until fork tender.
20-30 minutes.
• Drain potatoes in a strainer, and allow to cool.
• In a bowl, mix cooled potatoes, roasted red pepper sauce, ¾ cup of tomatoes,
¾ cup red onions, & 2 tbsp of parsley.
• Place in serving bowl, & garnish with remaining onions, tomatoes, and parsley.

## CHEF'S SUGGESTIONS:

*This dish can also be garnished with paprika and hard boiled eggs for a more traditional finish. I suggest serving this with the Spatchcock Harissa Cthicken. (see page 15)*

# Roasted Red Pepper Sauce

### Ingredients

- 1 cup of mayo
- 1 tbsp Dijon mustard
- 1 tbsp stone ground mustard
- 1 tbsp worstershire sauce
- ½ tsp chipotle pepper powder
- 2 tbsp honey
- ½ tsp ground cumin
- ½ tsp granulated garlic
- ½ tsp smoked sweet paprika
- 1 tbsp salt
- 1 tbsp coarse ground black pepper
- 3 oz roasted, peeled, & seeded red bell peppers (fresh or jar)

Directions
• Combine all ingredients in a blender andt blend until smooth.

**CHEF'S SUGGESTIONS:**

*This sauce can be used as a dressing for a salads, on sandwiches, as well as a dip for veggies & meats.*

# Salsa Verde

### Ingredients

- 4 cloves garlic, rough chopped
- 1 cup parsley, rough chopped
- 2 tbsp kosher salt
- 1 tsp red pepper flakes
- 1 cup of olive oil

**CHEF'S SUGGESTIONS:**

*This sauce is great on chicken, fish, steak, grilled vegetables, & shrimp. It also serves great as a marinade or finishing sauce.*

Directions
• Combine lime juice, salt and garlic in a blender. Allow to sit for 10 minutes.
• Add parsley, pepper flakes, and olive. Blender for 30 to 45 seconds.
• Let sauce stand for 30 min before serving. Mix well before using.

# Southwest Grilled Shrimp & Kale Salad

# Southwest Grilled Shrimp & Kale Salad

**Ingredients (Yields 2 Servings)**

*for salad*
- 3 cups of shredded kale
- ¼ cup of finely shredded red cabbage
- ¼ cup shredded carrots
- ¼ cup canned black beans, rinsed & drained
- ¼ cup canned corn, rinsed & drained
- ½ cup roasted red pepper sauce (see page 11)

*for shrimp*
- 1 pound jumbo tiger shrimp
- 1 tbsp salsa verde (see page 11)
- Salt & pepper to taste

## CHEF'S SUGGESTIONS:

*This recipe can also be substituted with chicken steak, or fish. Cook times will vary. You can also use fresh corn, roasted on the grill to level up the flavor.*

Directions *for salad*
• Combine all ingredients in a bowl and mix. Reserve 2 tbsp of roasted red pepper sauce for garnish.

Directions *for shrimp*
• Make sure shrimp are peeled & deveined.
• Marinate shrimp and skewer shrimp once through the top & once through the tail.
• Grill shrimp on a medium hot grill until shrimp turn pink, and are fully cooked through. 6-7 min.
• Place cooked shrimp on top of kale salad, drizzle with roasted red pepper sauce, & cilantro for garnish.

# Spatchcock
# Harissa Chicken

# Spatchcock Harissa Chicken

## Ingredients (Yields 2 Servings)

*Spice Rub Ingredients*
- 3 tablespoons of Harissa
- 1/2 tablespoon of Paprika
- 1/2 tablespoon of cumin
- 1/2 tablespoon of onion powder
- 1/2 tablespoon of garlic powder
- 1 tablespoon of curry
- ½ teaspoon of chipotle powder
- ½ teaspoon of cinnamon
- 1 teaspoon of Ground Mustard
- 1 teaspoon of salt
- 1 teaspoon of pepper
- 1 tablespoon of dark brown sugar
- 1/3 of cup of olive oil
- Combine all ingredients to
  make marinade for chicken

## CHEF'S SUGGESTIONS:

*This dish pairs with salads, or rice & your favorite vegetable. This marinade can be used with boneless/skinless chicken breast to make tacos or fajitas. You can substitute fish, pork, shrimp or beef with this marinade. Cook times will vary.*

Directions
• Turn whole chicken breast side down

• Use kitchen shears to cut alongside both sides of the backbone and remove

• Cut chicken through breastbone and sternum, without cutting through the meat, to lay chicken flat

• Use 1tablespoon of marinade per pound of chicken, marinate for at least 30 minutes up to overnight

• Cook indirectly on low-medium grill for 45min-1 hour or until chicken reaches 165 degrees internally.

• Allow chicken to rest for 10 minutes before cutting.

CHEF MARLO

# YOU SEE *the* FLAVOR

COOKBOOK VOL.1

CPSIA information can be obtained
at www.ICGtesting.com
Printed in the USA
BVHW020732240221
600911BV00012B/882